THE KOOKY KIDS GUIDE TO

BLACK AND WHITE

MONSTER

MOVIES

Also available from Joey Draper:

Twisted Tales for Kooky Kids:

Fangs Very Much

Ashlyn Goes to Wolf Mountain

Doctor's Orders

The Goo from Outer Space

Sea No Evil

Poetry:

Spooky Stories for Kooky Kids

This book is dedicated to the all the creatures, beasts and monsters that graced my television set and haunted my dreams.

THE KOOKY KIDS GUIDE TO
BLACK AND WHITE MONSTER MOVIES

written & illustrated by Joey Draper

published by
Kooky Kids Publishing

CONTENTS

GLOSSARY

Here you'll find a list of words and phrases relating to monster movies.

Abominable - hateful, disgusting and horrible.

B-Movie - a film made on a small budget.

Clairvoyant - a person who claims to have a supernatural ability to see into the future.

Colossal - large or huge.

Flick - an old-fashioned term for a film.

German Expressionism - an art style used in poetry and painting which is often discoloured and distorted to evoke emotions, moods and ideas.

Kaiju - Japanese for "strange beast", the term is used for large monsters such as Godzilla and King Kong.

Stop-Motion Animation - a technique used by moving an inanimate object between photographs to give the appearance of movement when the photographs are viewed in sequence.

A BRIEF INTRODUCTION

Whether it's Godzilla destroying Tokyo or Frankenstein's monster lurching around the doctor's lab, everyone can probably think of at least one iconic black and white movie monster.

The creatures designed for these age-old masterpieces have gone on to influence all sorts of things in modern culture, from animated movies to video games to breakfast cereal mascots. The whole world is subliminally aware of their existence.

However, with the abundance of remakes, sequels and reboots nowadays, it's easy to forget where all these beautifully bizarre creatures came from.

Growing up, black and white films were pretty much all I watched, along with a healthy dose of Saturday morning cartoons. I was certainly the odd one out in school. While everyone else was hooked on the TV shows of the time, I was watching the Amazing Colossal Man throw a giant syringe into an army corporal.

I personally found a lot of my joy in the sci-fi creature features of the nineteen fifties. Back then technology was advancing, space exploration was on the horizon and the fear of atomic radiation was very real. Out of that anxiety and panic came an abundance of incredibly creative and original scripts featuring a slew of magnificent aliens, monsters and beasts.

To this day, my childhood memories of watching monster movies with my dad are some of my fondest.

Yes, the special effects are outdated, the acting isn't always perfect and some of the monsters are utterly ridiculous, but there's just something about them.

Luckily, due to their age, many of the old monster movies are now rated as Parental Guidance. The lack of blood, bad language and violence makes them the perfect viewing for any kooky kid wanting a blast from the spooky past.

This book serves as a guide to the charming and somewhat forgotten world of black and white monster movies, hoping to ignite a new generation of diehard fans and expand the knowledge of those who've already been diagnosed with a bad case of monster mania.

So, grab your popcorn, turn out the lights and prepare for a scare.

APES OF WRATH

When you think of old movies starring big monsters, one of the first creatures that may spring to mind is King Kong. Billed at somewhere between eighteen and three-hundred feet tall, the Skull Island resident has featured in multiple movies. As well as his illustrious film career, King Kong has also featured in television shows, cartoons and video games. Although certainly the largest in some of his later outings, King Kong is not the only simian to grace the monstrous silver screen.

THE WHITE GORILLA - 1945

"Its hate for anything that walks makes it a deadly enemy."

This American-made film tells the tale of an albino gorilla cast out by its species due to its colour.

The white gorilla has become angry in its loneliness and, in turn, is a threat to all natives and explorers.

After an injured explorer by the name of Steve Collins crawls his way to a nearby trading post, he tells the tale of his run-in with the legendary White Gorilla.

Fun Facts:

A large portion of the film is made up of footage from a 1927 silent film named *Perils of the Jungle*.

THE APE MAN - 1943

Based on *They Creep in the Dark* by Karl Brown, this tale of an experiment gone wrong stars horror veteran Bela Lugosi.

It follows a talented photographer, Billy Mason, as she uncovers the dark mysteries of Dr James Brewster's accidental transformation.

Fun Facts:

In the United Kingdom the film was released under the title *Lock Your Doors*.

The star of this movie, Bela Lugosi, found fame twelve years prior, playing his most iconic role - Count Dracula.

KING KONG - 1933

Kong, the eighth wonder of the world and probably the most famous simian to grace the silver screen. The 1933 movie sees Kong in his natural habitat of Skull Island, where he fights to protect actress, Ann Darrow from an onslaught of dinosaur attacks.

After an explosive battle with American sailors, Kong is plucked from his home and taken to New York City. Sadly, the King of the Beasts isn't a fan of being exhibited.

Fun Facts:

The film uses a combination of puppetry, stop-motion animation and practical effects by Willis O'Brien. Willis went on to inspire Ray Harryhausen, who to this day is considered to be the best stop-motion animator of all time.

💀 THE KONG SCALE 💀

Kong's height across the vast array of remakes and reboots has certainly seen some changes. Here's a diagram of the King of the Beasts' growth over the years:

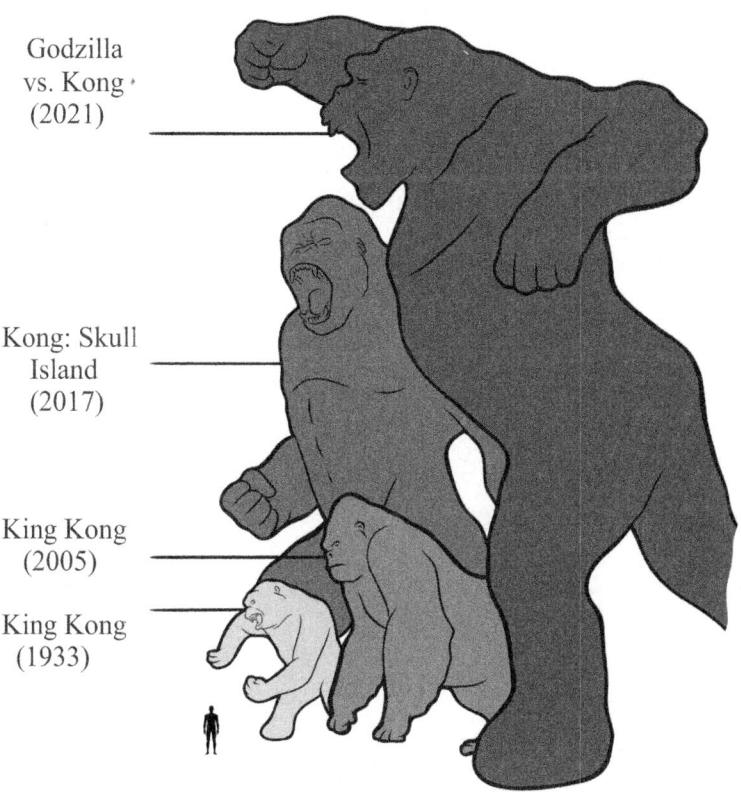

Godzilla
vs. Kong
(2021)

Kong: Skull
Island
(2017)

King Kong
(2005)

King Kong
(1933)

BRIDE OF THE GORILLA - 1951

"These are not my hands, not my arms, not my eyes.

That's not my face."

     Not all ape-like monsters are born that way. In this shocking B-movie horror, murderer Barney Chavez finds himself under the curse of a native witch called Al-Long. The curse forces him to turn into a monstrous gorilla-like beast when the dark of night approaches.

Fun Facts:

Although credited under his father's name, the detective investigating the murder is played by Lon Chaney Jr. This incredible actor played the 1941 version of the Wolf Man.

The entire movie was filmed in just ten days.

WHITE PONGO - 1945

In the very same year *The White Gorilla* was released, horror fans were treated to another albino gorilla flick in the form of *White Pongo*.

White Pongo tells the tale of a group of anthropologists searching for the white gorilla in an effort to prove it as the missing link between humans and monkeys.

Fun Facts:

The albino gorilla costume used for *White Pongo* was later recycled for the Abominable Snowman in the 1956 Himalayan horror *Man Beast*.

THE APE - 1940

"Hey, Doc, What are you gonna do to me?"

"I'm going to write you into medical history."

Horror icon Boris Karloff's first entry in this guide is 1940's *The Ape*. This horror/mystery tells the tale of the unethical Dr Adrian and his quest to cure a woman of her illness using unorthodox measures. When a large ape escapes from the nearby circus during a fire, it gives Dr Adrian the perfect cover story for gathering his unwilling donors.

Fun Facts:

The screenwriter of this film, Curt Siodmak, also penned 1956's *Earth vs. the Flying Saucers*, 1951's *Bride of the Gorilla* and 1941's *The Wolf Man*.

SON OF KONG - 1933

A direct sequel to King Kong, this film was released soon after its predecessor. *Son of Kong* sees the return of actors Robert Armstrong and Frank Reicher, as well as special effects guru Willis O'Brien.

Carl Denham and a handful of others return to Skull Island to find treasure, only to discover the son of Kong, cutely nicknamed "Little Kong".

Fun Facts:

King Kong and the residents of Skull Island are often classed as kaiju, a Japanese term associated with giant monsters.

Little Kong isn't the only offspring of a kaiju. In 1967 Minilla starred as the son of Godzilla.

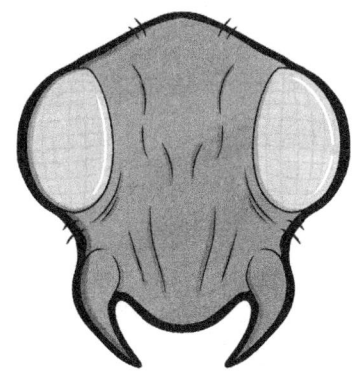

CREEPY CRAWLIES

Something icky this way comes! The nineteen-fifties saw an influx of creepy crawlies swarm their way onto the silver screen. Spiders, ants and even a praying mantis became the horrors for a new generation of horror fanatics.

Whether it's a fifty foot black scorpion or an army of grasshoppers, nuclear waste and radiation certainly had a lot to answer for. In this chapter we'll explore the insect infestation that truly got under everybody's skin.

THEM! - 1954

"There was enough formic acid in him to kill twenty men!"

Atomic ants paved the way for small insects getting big and taking over the box office. The success of this icky picture led to it being one of the highest grossing films of the year for Warner Bros.

Them! warns of the aftermath of atomic bombs in an explosive and exhilarating way, pitting man against giant insect in a battle to save New Mexico.

Fun Facts:

Star Trek actor Leonard Nimoy has a brief role within the film.

The study of ants is called Myrmecology.

TARANTULA - 1955

If first-person spider attacks and a giant black tarantula taking on the entire town's police force appeals to you, then this is the movie for you.

After a doctor's experiment escapes the lab, a trail of bones leads the police to the discovery of the ever-growing genetically modified tarantula.

The film was directed by Jack Arnold, famous for *Creature from the Black Lagoon* and *It Came from Outer Space*. With the backing of Universal Pictures, the film is highly regarded for its special effects and box-office success.

Fun Facts:

There are around nine hundred species of tarantula. They live on every continent, except Antartica, due to their love for tropical and subtropical climates.

BEGINNING OF THE END - 1957

If ants and spiders can be successful, then why not grasshoppers? That was seemingly the thought process behind this creature feature.

When it is discovered the village of Ludlow, Illinois, has been destroyed and its residents are missing, the entire area is sealed off to the public.

A journalist's investigation leads her to the U.S. Department of Agriculture, where she meets Dr Ed Wainwright, an agricultural scientist working on creating giant fruit and vegetables through radiation. Together they uncover the truth of the giant man-eating locusts.

Fun Facts:

Dr Ed Wainwright is played by Peter Graves, who also starred in *It Conquered the World* along with the highly comedic *Airplane* movies.

EARTH VS. THE SPIDER - 1958

While searching for her missing father, Carol Flynn and her boyfriend Mike stumble across a giant spider living within an abandoned cave. Naturally the town's sheriff doesn't believe them, but when a kind-hearted professor suggests they might be telling the truth an investigation is set in motion.

Although they think they have destroyed the beast, the giant spider is free to wreak havoc upon the town in full B-movie fashion.

Fun Facts:

The spider seen within this movie is actually a real live tarantula, superimposed into the picture and scaled up to appear gigantic.

Due to the success of *The Fly* in 1958, the film was temporarily marketed as simply, *The Spider*.

HORRORS OF SPIDER ISLAND - 1960

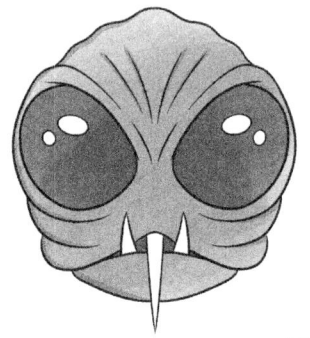

This West German horror flick shows that not all spider bites are equal. After a catastrophic plane crash leaves a nightclub manager and his dancers stranded on an island, he is bitten by a giant spider.

Long before the tales of Peter Parker and his spider-like super powers, Gary Webster (yes, they really put "web" in his surname) is transformed into a hideous man-spider hybrid.

Fun Facts:

The German title of this film is *Ein Toter hing im Netz* (A Corpse Hung in a Web).

Most of the scenes were filmed in Yugoslavia.

THE DEADLY MANTIS - 1957

"In the kingdom of the living, there is no more deadly or voracious creature than the praying mantis."

After a volcanic eruption a giant praying mantis, trapped for millions of years, is freed from its icy tomb. The colossal beast makes its way from the secluded and snowy region of Northern Canada to the highly populated Washington D.C. and New York areas. In its newfound surroundings the deadly mantis leaves a trail of death and unbelievable destruction.

Fun Facts:

Although slow and cumbersome in this movie, praying mantises are actually incredibly agile and can jump with extreme precision.

MONSTER FROM GREEN HELL - 1957

By the time *Monster from the Green Hell* was released there was certainly a buzz about the giant insect sub-genre. This buzzing only got louder with the introduction of giant mutant wasps caused by cosmic radiation.

A change of scenery from most of the big bug movies, *Monster from the Green Hell* takes place in Africa, where a rocket holding the mutated test subjects has crash landed.

After several reports of gigantic monsters in Central Africa, Dr Brady travels there to try to put a stop to his scientific catastrophe.

Fun Facts:

Dr Lorentz was played by Russian actor Vladimir Sokoloff, who also had roles in *I Was a Teenage Werewolf* and *The Twilight Zone*.

THE WASP WOMAN - 1959

From mutated wasps to a wasp woman. This American movie, also known as *The Bee Girl*, tells the tale of Janice Starlin. Janice is the owner of a cosmetics company but, due to her natural aging, her customers are starting to lose faith in her products.

Hoping to make herself younger, Janice injects herself with a prototype formula made from the royal jelly of a queen wasp. Sadly, this has monstrous results.

Fun Facts:

The Wasp Woman was produced and directed by horror legend Roger Corman. Corman is responsible for *Creature from the Haunted Sea*, *Attack of the Crab Monsters*, *A Bucket of Blood*, *The Pit and the Pendulum*, *Teenage Caveman* and the original *Little Shop of Horrors* to name a few.

RETURN OF THE FLY - 1958

Although the original Fly movie was released in colour, its two sequels, *Return of the Fly* and *Curse of the Fly*, were both released in black and white.

The first sequel stars horror great and co-star of the original, Vincent Price. It follows the son of the original Fly as he tries to perfect his father's teleportation pods. Sadly, a backstabbing lab partner tries to sabotage the project.

Fun Facts:

Nearly ten per cent of the entire movie's budget went on Vincent Price's acting fee. Luckily, this incredible actor was worth every penny.

💀 THE TALENTED MR PRICE 💀

Whether you know Vincent Price from his films, television appearances, or for his distinctive voice on Michael Jackson's *Thriller*, there is no doubting this man's talents.

Born in 1911, Price went on to star in over one hundred films, a large portion of them horror and science fiction.

His terrifying laugh, well-spoken voice and theatrical performances made his roles some of the most memorable and truly frightening.

I remember seeing *House on Haunted Hill* for the first time. During the introduction we see the house and Vincent Price's ghostly head floating towards the camera.

At the time, I had only seen Vincent Price as Eggman in the 1960s Batman TV series. As brilliant as this campy performance was, it didn't show "The Master of Horror" in his true terrifying form.

I sat, mouth ajar, as the ghostly head of Vincent Price introduced himself as Frederick Loren. His short speech informs the audience of his wife's haunted house party.

The friendly eyes, moustached smile and warm tone are almost poetically sinister as he speaks of ghosts and murder.

With a myriad of horrors under his belt, Vincent Price is rightly celebrated as one of the greats, along with the likes of Christopher Lee, Peter Cushing and Boris Karloff.

He has two stars on the Hollywood Walk of Fame for film and television.

His last on-screen performance was as The Inventor in Tim Burton's *Edward Scissorhands*. Price sadly passed away on October 25th 1993 at the age of eighty-two.

CURSE OF THE FLY - 1965

"You're not God, you're not even human!"

In this British-made sequel Patricia, a young woman escaping from a mental institution, accidentally meets a descendant of the original Fly. Patricia and Martin Delambre get married, but Martin holds a secret curse brought on by his family's experiments.

Unbeknownst to Patricia, this isn't the only secret Martin's family is hiding. Locked away, out of sight, are the failed test subjects and their horrifying disfigurements.

Fun Facts:

Just four years prior to this film, actor Carole Gray, who played Patricia, was in a musical with rock n' roll singer Cliff Richard.

THE BLACK SCORPION - 1957

This Mexican-American movie used the talents of Willis O'Brien, famed for his work on 1933's King Kong.

Much like *The Deadly Mantis*, the monsters of this movie are released during a natural disaster. This time around it's an earthquake that causes a volcanic eruption, which in turn releases giant prehistoric scorpions. The nearby residents must investigate their nest and find their weak spot before the black scorpion makes its way to Mexico City.

Fun Facts:

The original poster for this movie gave the cinema the right to turn the lights up if at any time the audience became too emotionally disturbed by what they were watching.

THE STRANGE WORLD OF PLANET X - 1958

Independently made, this British sci-fi horror was also known as *Cosmic Monsters*.

It tells the story of an obsessed scientist disrupting the Earth's magnetic field during his experiments. The knock-on effects of this not only attract alien lifeforms, they also cause blasts of cosmic radiation.

As a result, the Earth's insects and spiders transform into gigantic man-eating monsters. Aliens and humans must unite before the world is destroyed.

Fun Facts:

Lead actor Forrest Tucker also starred in *The Crawling Eye* and *The Abominable Snowman* with Hammer Horror veteran Peter Cushing.

TEENAGE TERRORS

In the late fifties, movie makers realised that a large number of teenagers were flocking to the cinemas to see these monstrous creature features. Thus, the dawn of the teenage monster epic was upon us.

Over a short two year period a slew of horror flicks aimed at troublesome teens was released, hoping to cash in on the horror-crazed high schoolers… and believe me, acne is the least of these kids' worries.

I WAS A TEENAGE FRANKENSTEIN - 1957

Taking a very large leaf out of Mary Shelley's book, this American film tells the tale of Professor Frankenstein collecting body parts to create a monster.

Using the body from a horrendous car accident, the professor is inevitably successful in his creation of one of the creepiest-looking villains to grace the silver screen.

With a string of murders in order to find the monster a less grotesque face, Dr Karlton must try to stop the infernal beast.

Fun Facts:

This film influenced shock rocker Alice Cooper and his guitarist Kane Roberts to write *Teenage Frankenstein* from the 1986 album *Constrictor*. The song featured on the soundtrack to *Friday The 13th Part VI: Jason Lives*.

TEENAGE CAVEMAN - 1958

Starring celebrated actor Robert Vaughn, this "prehistoric" horror is set in a barren wasteland. The land is separated from lush, plant-filled grounds by a river and an age-old law.

The story of an ancient god that lurks along the riverbank and kills any man with a single touch is in every caveman's mind.

The titular teenage caveman, known only as the Symbol Maker's son, defies the law and crosses the river with his friends, only to discover the terrifying truth of the tale.

Fun Facts:

A low-budget remake of this film was released in 2002 starring Andrew Keegan, who featured in the movies *Independence Day* and *10 Things I Hate About You*.

I WAS A TEENAGE WEREWOLF - 1957

Taking the form of a werewolf for this high school horror is Michael Landon, most famously known for his long-running role as Charles Ingalls in *Little House on the Prairie*.

I Was a Teenage Werewolf tells the tale of an angry teen in need of professional help. That help unfortunately comes in the form of Dr Brandon.

Tricking the troubled teen, Dr Brandon injects him with an experimental serum and the results are hair-raising.

Fun Facts:

This film features in Stephen King's *IT* as well as its nineties TV movie adaptation.

TEENAGE ZOMBIES - 1959

Curious teenagers Reg, Skip, Julie and Pam accidentally discover an island while out water-skiing. The island is run by Dr Myra, a female and incredibly mad scientist who plans to turn everyone in the United States into zombies.

The teenagers are captured by Dr Myra's pet zombie, Ivan, and thrown into cages. They must find a way to escape the evil doctor's basement and get off this mysterious island.

Fun Facts:

The term *teenager* didn't start being used until 1944. It was invented by marketing executives to recognise the spending power of adolescents and differentiate between younger and older children.

TEENAGERS FROM OUTER SPACE - 1959

"We are the supreme race. We have the

supreme weapons."

An alien race is looking for somewhere to raise its food source, giant creatures named Gargons. Sadly, planet Earth seems to be the perfect place.

Luckily for the humans, one alien, Derek, and his earthling girlfriend, Betty, are determined to stop the aliens from succeeding in their plan.

The aliens are pretty brutal in this film and end up vaporising many of the residents, including Betty's poor dog, Sparky.

Fun Facts:

Robert 'King' Moody played the alien spacecraft captain. He also played the McDonalds mascot Ronald in all of their TV commercials from 1969 until 1985.

💀 MONSTROUS MELODIES 💀

Here are some of the horror-related songs the teenagers were listening to back when these monster movies were released.

I Put a Spell On You by Screamin' Jay Hawkins

Monster Mash by Boris Pickett & The Crypt Kickers

The Gila Monster by Joe Johnson

Race with the Devil by Gene Vincent

The Head Hunters by Mike Fern

Jekyll And Hyde by Jim Burgett

Frankenstein's Den by The Hollywood Flames

Graveyard Rock by Tarantula Ghoul & Her Gravediggers

The Monster Hop by Jimmy Dee & The Meteors

Werewolf by The Frantics

First Man on Mars by Jackie Fautheree

Vampira by Bobby Bare

SILENT BUT DEADLY

One of the most intriguing and charming eras of cinema is the age of the silent film. The hand-wound cameras meant the speed of the film wandered freely. This, coupled with the flickering projectors and scratched film, adds an abundance of character, mystique and overall creepiness to the footage.

Going back to where it all began, these are some of the earliest examples of horror captured on film.

FRANKENSTEIN - 1910

With an original runtime of just sixteen minutes, this silent horror is believed to be the first onscreen adaptation of Mary Shelley's famous novel.

The film was produced by inventor Thomas Edison, famed for inventing the phonograph, the motion picture camera and early versions of the electric light bulb.

Even at this early stage of filmmaking various special effect techniques are used with chilling results.

It shows the doctor's creation of the perfect human, his disgust at its evil appearance and his fight to keep his new bride safe.

Fun Facts:

The ending of this silent film differs greatly to that of Mary Shelley's novel.

DR JEKYLL AND MR HYDE - 1920

An adaptation of Scottish author Robert Louis Stevenson's *The Strange Case of Dr Jekyll and Mr Hyde* comes in the form of this silent masterpiece.

The 1920 version of this gothic tale stars John Barrymore who, due to his distinguished features, was nicknamed 'The Great Profile'.

The film follows Dr Jekyll as he accidentally releases a vicious alter ego by the name of Mr Hyde. The make-up and look of the film create an incredibly memorable and hauntingly creepy villain for the silent era.

Fun Facts:

Actor John Barrymore is the grandfather of Drew Barrymore, who starred in the horror films *Scream*, *Firestarter* and *Cat's Eye*.

THE PHANTOM OF THE OPERA - 1925

The star of this silent film, Lon Chaney Sr., was known as "The Man of a Thousand Faces". This talented actor and make-up artist brought Gaston Leroux's phantom character to life in a vivid and petrifying way.

In this classic telling, singer Christine is haunted by a mysterious voice telling her to think only of her career.

The phantom haunts the Paris Opera House, causing all sorts of mischief and mayhem. This and the famed unmasking of the phantom have led this to be a chilling rendition.

Fun Facts:

During early screenings of the film it was reported that people were seen screaming and fainting during the now infamous unmasking scene.

💀 THE MANY FACES OF LON CHANEY SR 💀

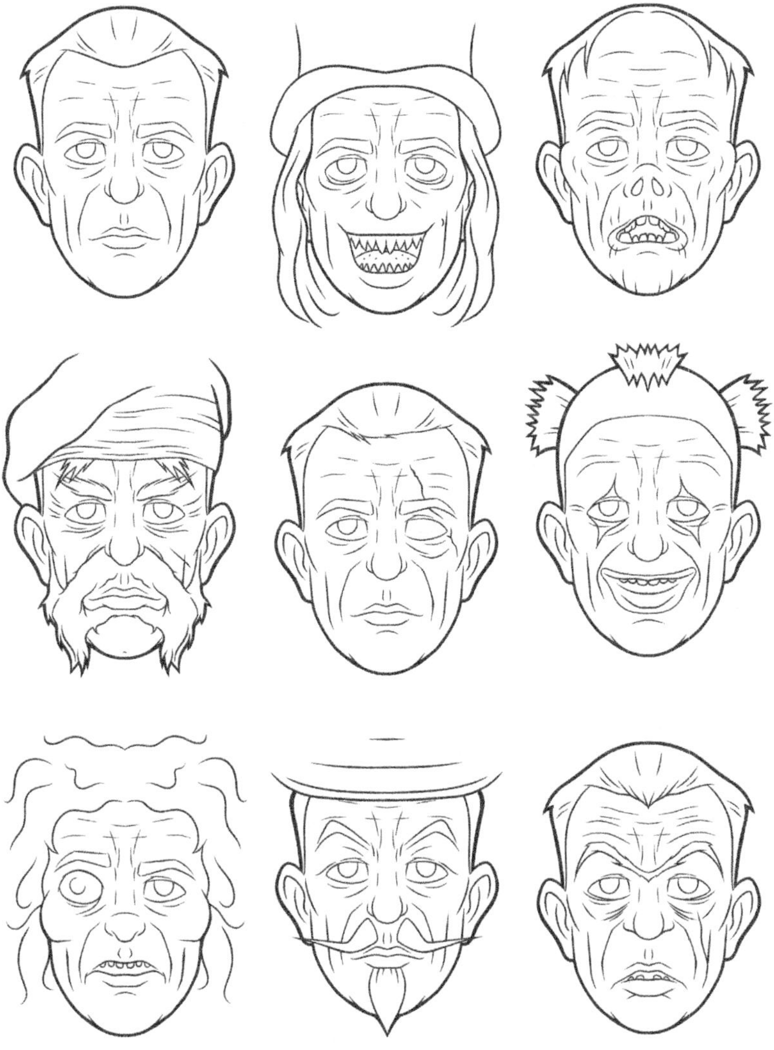

My first encounter with Lon Chaney Sr. was simply a photograph in a horror book. The photo was a still from *London After Midnight*, in which Lon Chaney Sr. plays a vampire known as "The Man in the Beaver Hat".

The sharpened teeth, drooping eyes and maniacal grin sent shivers up my spine. To this day, the make-up, which Chaney did himself, is still some of the scariest I have ever seen.

Born in 1883, Chaney was applauded for his acting range and his ability to play afflicted and grotesque characters with power and sincerity.

Sadly, due to their age, many of Chaney's films are considered lost, but "The Man of a Thousand Faces" appeared in over one hundred and fifty during his career.

Chaney sadly died on August 26th, 1930 at the age of just forty-seven.

NOSFERATU - 1922

Max Schreck stars as Count Orlok in this German vampire film. The movie is actually an unofficial and unauthorised adaptation of Bram Stoker's novel *Dracula*.

An estate agent makes his way to Count Orlok's castle to sell him an isolated house in Wisbourg.

During his stay the estate agent notices strange behaviour from the count and an abundance of evidence that points to acts of vampirism.

Fun Facts:

The film was banned in Sweden until 1972 for its depiction of excessive horror.

Tim Burton used the name Max Schreck for Christopher Walken's character in *Batman Returns*.

THE GOLEM - 1915

Staying in Germany, *The Golem* is a partially-lost film about an antiques dealer who accidentally stumbles across a golem.

The golem is a clay statue, made and brought to life to protect the Jewish people against persecution. The antiques dealer awakens the golem to exploit it for his own ends; however, when the golem sees the dealer's daughter, Jessica, he is helplessly in love.

Jessica doesn't return these feelings, and the golem goes on an uncontrollable rampage.

Fun Facts:

Shortly after its release, the film was considered lost. Although some partial edits exist, the film has not been seen in its entirety since 1915. It's a shame as it is considered to be the first ever monster movie.

THE CABINET OF DR CALIGARI - 1920

One of the most famous silent films of all time, and often applauded as the quintessential example of German expressionism.

The film tells the story of an insane hypnotist who uses his sleepwalking servant, Cesare, to carry out acts of murder.

The film uses painted canvas and backdrops to create a twisted town of distorted angular streets and rooftops. With an equally twist-filled script, *The Cabinet of Dr. Caligari* is a must-see.

Fun Facts:

The film pioneered non-linear storytelling, using flashbacks to add complexity and disorientation.

THE HUNCHBACK OF NOTRE DAME - 1923

In this film Lon Chaney Sr. plays Quasimodo, a deaf and hunchbacked bell-ringer for the Notre Dame cathedral.

Led by his evil master, Jehan, the hunchback kidnaps Esmerelda, a Roma girl living in Paris. After Esmerelda is rescued, Quasimodo is sentenced to be publicly lashed in the square.

Feeling sorry for the hunchback, Esmerelda and Archdeacon Dom Claude put a stop to Quasimodo's punishment and look to bring his master's wicked ways to an end.

Fun Facts:

The Hunchback of Notre Dame was Universal's most successful silent film. Chaney's performance was described as "a marvel of sympathetic acting" by Motion Picture World.

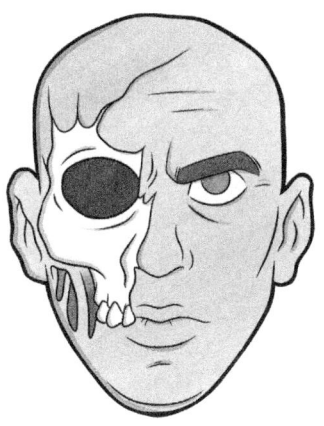

GIANTS AND LITTLE PEOPLE

In the late fifties it wasn't just insects and apes that were growing to humungous sizes. Moviegoers were treated to some pretty awesome special effects for the time, making giant humans the villains of the big screen.

Not only were humans given the growth treatment, but some of these movies shrank our heroes and audiences down to the size of an ant.

The next chapter delves into the world of big performances and little roles.

THE AMAZING COLOSSAL MAN - 1957

"I don't wanna grow anymore!"

During the test of the new plutonium bomb, Army Colonel, Glenn Manning, is exposed to a mass of radiation. Luckily the blast doesn't kill him, but it does have an unfortunate side effect.

Glenn begins to grow at a rapid rate, slowly losing his mind in the process. The film shows the agonising mental hardship of his uncontrollable condition.

Soon enough the entire city bears witness to the amazing colossal man's destructive power.

Fun Facts:

Veteran horror actor Dick Miller was considered for the role of Glenn Manning. Dick Miller's credits include *Gremlins*, *The Terminator*, *Piranha*, *Night of the Creeps* and *Chopping Mall*.

ATTACK OF THE PUPPET PEOPLE - 1958

Starring June Kenney from *Earth vs. The Spider*, this film tells the story of an evil puppet master named Mr Franz.

June Kenney plays newly-recruited secretary Sally Reynolds. Early on in her career at Dolls, Inc. she meets Bob (played by John Agar from *The Mole People*, *Tarantula* and *The Brain from Planet Arous*).

When Bob goes missing and a new doll that looks suspiciously like him appears in Mr Franz's collection, Sally starts to think he may be shrinking people.

Fun Facts:

Director Bert I. Gordon was also responsible for directing *Beginning of the End*, *Earth vs. The Spider*, *The Amazing Colossal Man* and its sequel, *War of the Colossal Beast*.

ATTACK OF THE 50 FOOT WOMAN - 1958

Nancy Archer is driving down a desert road when she encounters an alien spacecraft. The alien pilot grabs at her, but she manages to escape.

No one believes her story due to her drinking problem, but another encounter with the alien leaves Nancy poisoned with radiation.

As a result Nancy begins to grow, giving her all the power to enact vengeance on her cheating husband and his mistress.

Fun Facts:

Allison Hayes, who played the fifty-foot woman, also acted alongside Elvis Presley in the film *Tickle Me*.

THE INCREDIBLE SHRINKING MAN - 1957

"In my hunt for food I had become the hunted."

Based on the novel *The Shrinking Man*, this movie tells the tale of Scott, who exposed to a strange mist while on holiday. This, coupled with exposure to a pesticide, rearranges his molecular structure and begins the shrinking process.

As he fights to stop and reverse the shrinking process his mental health deteriorates. With his hopes of returning to normal dwindling, Scott finds himself battling with the press, seclusion and even his own cat.

Fun Facts:

Scott's cat was played by a trained cat named Orangey, who also had roles in *This Island Earth* and *The Comedy of Terrors*.

WAR OF THE COLOSSAL BEAST - 1958

A sequel to *The Amazing Colossal Man*, this movie picks up right where its predecessor left off.

Although none of the original cast returned, director of *The Amazing Colossal Man*, Bert I. Gordon, returned to lead the project as writer, producer and director.

Glenn, who is believed to have died at the Hoover Dam, is horribly disfigured and mentally traumatised. He has made his way to Mexico and is hiding in the mountains.

The U.S. Army captures Glenn and brings him back to the United States. Sadly, Glenn escapes and sets off on a rampage through Los Angeles.

Fun Facts:

The character of Glenn Manning only says one word throughout the entirety of the movie.

GIANT FROM THE UNKNOWN - 1958

In true Frankenstein fashion, a lightning bolt is what causes this next beast to awaken, this time in the form of a giant Spanish conqueror named Vargas.

Giant from the Unknown follows a group of scientists as they try to uncover the mystery of a murder and mutilated livestock.

After he is disturbed from his eternal slumber, Vargas looks to hunt down the scientists, along with any other living creature that stands in his way.

Fun Facts:

Jacob Baer, who played Vargas, was a boxer. He had fifty-seven wins, with fifty-four by knockout.

The make-up was created by Jack Pierce, who worked on Universal's *Frankenstein* and *The Mummy*.

UNDERWATER ANOMOLIES

Did you know that we know more about outer space that we do about the deep dark depths of our own oceans?

Who knows what could be lurking down there? Could there really be an ancient sea creature like Gill-man waiting to attack the humans?

A string of monster movies in the fifties and sixties tried to answer this question. In this chapter we'll explore the beasts that crawled out from the depths and stomped their slimy feet on solid land.

IT CAME FROM BENEATH THE SEA - 1955

"The next time I cruise in these waters I'm going to have torpedoes with warheads on them."

A navy submarine picks up traces of an underwater creature. Commander Pete Mathews and a team of scientists look to uncover the mystery of this seemingly giant sea beast.

Huge tentacles are seen, and with reports of missing vessels piling up, the threat of the hungry monstrosity moving to the city is becoming more likely.

Using the skills of Ray Harryhausen, the film manages to bring to life a giant radioactive octopus which attacks San Fransisco's Golden Gate Bridge.

Fun Facts:

To save on budget, Ray Harryhausen's radioactive octopus only had six tentacles.

ATTACK OF THE CRAB MONSTERS - 1959

Investigating the effects of nuclear weapons testing and an entire missing research team, a group of scientists becomes stranded on a remote island.

The island is slowly sinking into the sea, but sadly that is the least of their worries.

They soon discover the island is inhabited by intelligent giant crab monsters. One by one the crew meet their doom at the pincers of these murderous mutations. The survivors must stop these carnivorous crustaceans before there's no one left.

Fun Facts:

When breeding, female crabs lay anywhere between one and two thousand eggs. Crabs have ten legs and most of them walk and swim sideways. They communicate with their pincers by drumming and waving.

BEHEMOTH THE SEA MONSTER - 1959

This British-American creature feature, also known as *The Great Behemoth*, sees a resurrected dinosaur rampaging through the streets of London.

Radioactive waste and atomic testing strike again, this time causing a slew of radioactive blobs that threaten the ocean's ecosystem. When these changes suddenly awaken a prehistoric monster, Steve Karens and his band of professors must put a stop to the seemingly unstoppable force.

Fun Facts:

Many of the sound effects are taken from 1933's *King Kong*, including Fay Wray's scream.

THE HORROR OF PARTY BEACH - 1964

Partying at the beach is all well and good until a horde of gill-covered sea creatures decide to take a stroll on the sun-kissed sand.

The product of yet another radioactive waste dump, these fish-faced humanoids are out looking for flesh. The nearby beach party holds a wide variety of fresh meat and nothing is going to stand in their way.

Featuring one of the more interesting creature designs, this movie boasts a strange and unique set of monsters that is guaranteed to leave an impression.

Fun Facts:

The Horror of Party Beach features a lot of music. Adverts described it as the first horror monster musical. The band within the film was a real rock band, The Del-Aires.

CREATURE FROM THE BLACK LAGOON – 1954

One of the most famous sea creatures in the monster world, Gill-man is nothing short of a horror icon.

Not content with leaving the creature splashing about the Amazonian jungle, a group of scientists decides to try to capture it for their studies. Unfortunately for them, Gill-man has other ideas.

With the beautiful Julie Adams, breathtaking underwater scenes performed by Rico Browning and a memorable outcast of a monster, it is clear why *The Creature from the Black Lagoon* is remembered so fondly.

Fun Facts:

The film spawned two sequels. *Revenge of the Creature* (1955) and *The Creature Walks Among Us* (1956).

💀 CREATURE DESIGN BY MILICENT PATRICK 💀

Until recently, Milicent Patrick had gone uncredited and uncelebrated for her incredible design of Gill-man.

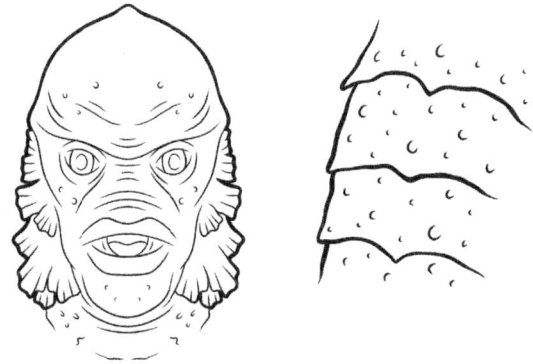

In a new book by Mallory O'Meara, *The Lady of the Black Lagoon*, the author celebrates this forgotten feminist trailblazer.

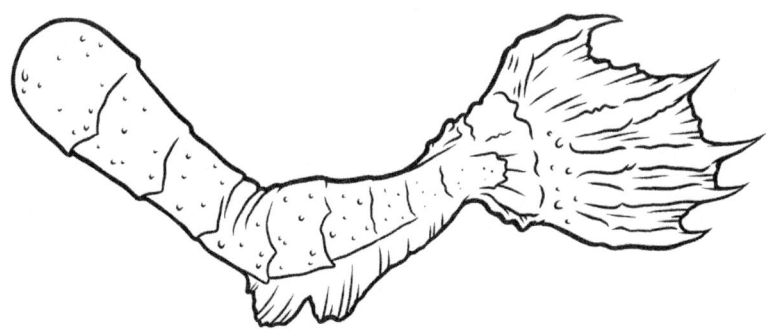

ATTACK OF THE GIANT LEECHES - 1959

A swamp is seemingly responsible for a rising number of disappearances and deaths.

The film tells the story of a game warden, a doctor, and their posse trying to uncover the mystery threatening their community.

With cheating partners, murder, and fifty dollars of reward money in the equation, the investigation takes a series of twists and turns.

The trail leads the warden and his men to a cave beneath the swamp, where giant leeches with a craving for human blood dwell.

Fun Facts:

In the past leeches were commonly used for medicinal purposes to extract toxins and clean wounds. They have ten eyes; however, their eyesight is still very bad.

THE MONSTER THAT CHALLENGED THE WORLD - 1957

Following a fierce earthquake, a chasm opens up beneath the sea, releasing a swarm of prehistoric molluscs.

Looking like a bulbous-eyed giant centipede, the creature in this flick is definitely one of the more terrifying beasts to crawl its way out of Hollywood.

Lieutenant Commander John Twillinger, or "Twill" for short, heads up a team to investigate a seemingly attacked ship. When they find the ship and its lifeless crew covered in slime, they know something strange is going on.

A battle between man and monster ensues to stop the destruction of planet Earth.

Fun Facts:

Popular Western actor Tim Holt came out of retirement to star in this monster movie. He only made two more films after this one.

CREATURE FROM THE HAUNTED SEA - 1961

"You made that monster up out of thin air!"

A crook has a diabolical scheme in which he will take people fleeing a Caribbean island in revolt onto his boat, kill them and blame it on a mythical monster.

I know what you're thinking, and you're absolutely right. This film is pretty much the first live-action version of a Scooby Doo episode. Except the bad guy isn't a henchman in a rubber mask, but the real life sea monster from the crook's tale.

With one of the more goofy-looking creatures, this film is still well worth a watch.

Fun Facts:

The film was shot in just five days and used local residents as extras, paying them one dollar a day.

MONSTER FROM THE OCEAN FLOOR - 1954

A supersized killer octopus is the fiend of choice in this American-made monster movie.

Set in a small Mexican village by the cove, the film tells the story of vacationer Julie and her sceptical marine biologist boyfriend, Steve, as they discover the ginormous beast lurking on the ocean floor.

This was the king of the B-movies, Roger Corman's first go at producing a film, and it certainly paid off.

Fun Facts:

The original title for this film was *It Stalked The Ocean Floor*.

VAMPIRES EVERYWHERE!

With razor sharp fangs and a lust for blood, vampires have become one of the most beloved monsters of all time.

With films like *The Lost Boys*, *Dracula Untold* and the *Twilight* series keeping this sub-genre alive, it's unlikely that vampires will be disappearing from our screens anytime soon.

In this chapter we'll be focusing on the movies that brought the undead bloodsuckers to the silver screen.

LONDON AFTER MIDNIGHT - 1927

This silent horror tells the story of Roger Balfour, a wealthy man who suddenly passes away. His death is investigated by Inspector Burke and considered to be by his own hand.

His mansion is left abandoned for five years, but when the locals start seeing movement and strange lights coming from the property, Inspector Burke is called back.

Now seemingly a dwelling place for vampiric creatures, Burke must navigate the mansion and uncover the mystery of Balfour's death.

After a fire at the Metro-Goldwyn-Meyer film vault, the film was official deemed lost.

Fun Facts:

The film was remade in 1935 as *Mark of the Vampire*.

THE VAMPIRE BAT - 1933

"Goodnight gentlemen. Don't let the vampires get you."

Paranoia and suspicion are high in the village of Klineschloss. The villagers are seemingly dying of blood loss, and all the evidence points to vampires.

When the simple-minded Herman Gleib is blamed due to his obsession with bats, the villagers form a mob. Chasing Herman and eventually forcing him to his death, the villagers hope that is the end of the murders.

Sadly for them, the vampiric attacks are only beginning.

Fun Facts:

The film re-used sets from 1931's *Frankenstein* to stay within budget.

CURSE OF THE UNDEAD - 1959

This horror western started out a bit of joke between husband-and-wife writing team Edward and Mildred Dein. Much to their shock, the team at Universal loved the idea and decided to shoot it.

The young women of a small western town are apparently dying of a disease that seems to drain their blood. Simultaneously an evil gunslinger with an aversion to sunlight has wandered into town.

A local preacher and his girlfriend must stop the vampiric cowboy before the whole town is drained of blood.

Fun Facts:

This movie is considered to be the first western to feature supernatural vampires. It influenced the 1966 films *Billy the Kid vs Dracula* and *Jesse James Meets Frankenstein's Daughter*.

VAMPYR - 1932

Danish director Carl Theodor Dreyer penned and directed this gothic horror.

The film makes full use of the title cards of the silent movie era. This was to keep talking to a minimum, as the film was being released in several languages.

The movie tells the tale of Allan Gray, a supernatural-obsessed drifter, as he stumbles across a village shrouded in mystery.

The village has all the markings of a vampire attack and, at the heart of it, a gravely ill woman name Léone.

Fun Facts:

The idea for the movie came from the success of the popular *Dracula* stage show. The director wanted to make something fashionable.

DRACULA - 1931

Universal's take on Bram Stoker's *Dracula* and its Broadway counterpart is a dark and atmospheric masterpiece.

The story follows Renfield as he meets with Dracula to discuss the purchase of a property in England. After a vicious attack, Renfield is now the Count's mindless slave.

Dracula makes his way to London and soon embarks on a feeding frenzy to quench his lust for blood.

All the while, Van Helsing is looking to prove the Count as a vampire and put an end to his tyranny.

Fun Facts:

Several actors were considered for the role of Dracula but, due to Lugosi's success on Broadway, he managed to get the part.

☠ THE HUNGARIAN HORROR, BELA LUGOSI ☠

Universal's *Dracula* was the first film I saw starring Bela. His performance is nothing short of inspiring in this production of the Bram Stoker's novel.

Lugosi was born in Hungary on October 20th, 1882. At just ten years old Lugosi took to the stage, and he appeared in over one hundred and seventy Hungarian productions.

In 1927 his stage performances moved to Broadway, where he took on the role of Count Dracula. This on-stage performance led to his casting in the Universal Pictures production.

Following the success of Dracula, Lugosi went on to appear in many horrors, such as *White Zombie*, *Son of Frankenstein* and *The Ape Man*.

He sadly passed away in 1956 of a heart attack. He was buried in his Dracula costume as well as one of his Dracula capes.

DRACULA'S DAUGHTER - 1936

"Thank you, I never drink... wine."

Universal's official sequel to *Dracula* picks up right where the original ended.

Professor Van Helsing has been arrested and sits in the cells of Scotland Yard. While he awaits his trial, a Hungarian Countess, Marya Zaleska, comes to London hoping to free herself of the vampiric curse she has had bestowed upon her.

Using her evil jewelled ring, she mesmerises her victims and gives in to her bloodlust. Van Helsing, together with the police, must try to stop the Countess before the body count grows.

Fun Facts:

This was one of Universal's most expensive films of the 1930s.

DEAD MEN WALK - 1945

A doctor named Lloyd Clayton is suspected of murdering his twin brother, Elwyn. He claims it was self-defence as his brother was dangerous due to his involvement in satanic occult practises and the dark arts.

It is this dark magic that brings Elwyn back to life as a vampiric creature who requires blood. Lloyd and his niece must find a way to kill Elwyn again, much to the dismay of Elwyn's hunchback assistant, Zolarr.

Fun Facts:

The film was shot in just six days and is one of the last films of actor Dwight Frye. Frye famously played Renfield in the 1931 version of *Dracula*.

THINGS YOU NEED DURING A DRAC ATTACK

Crucifix

Garlic

Sunlight

Holy Water

Stake

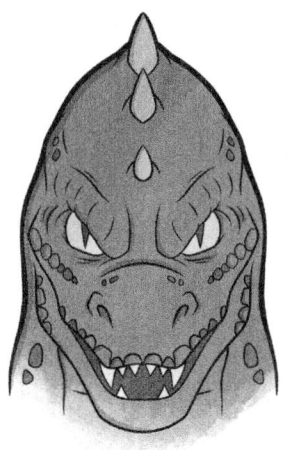

RAMPAGING REPTILES

Whether they are resurrected dinosaurs, mutated humans or creatures that have been in hiding, reptiles have played a huge part in the monster genre.

Ever since the beast from 20,000 fathoms thawed from its icy chamber, the world has been fascinated by prehistoric reptiles.

With destructive power like no other, this chapter looks at the lethal lizards and devastating dinosaurs of the creature feature era.

GODZILLA - 1954

Known as "The King of the Monsters", Godzilla is certainly up there with the greats. Having starred in over thirty five movies, this towering tyrant is a force to be reckoned with.

In the original Godzilla movie several ships have been destroyed. After investigating the attacks Professor Yamane spots a huge reptile the locals call Godzilla.

When Tokyo, along with a host of other Japanese cities, is under threat, Professor Yamane and his team must find a way to stop Godzilla in his tracks.

Fun Facts:

The actor in the Godzilla suit, Harou Nakajima, could only film for up to three minutes before he would overheat and pass out due to the suit's design.

THE SNAKE WOMAN - 1961

"That snake venom flowing through my blood, what will it do to my unborn child?"

In his infinite wisdom, a nineteenth century doctor injects his mentally ill wife with snake venom in an attempt to cure her.

After she gives birth to what the villagers call "The Devil's Baby", their family home is burned to the ground.

Years pass and suddenly there's a spate of murders involving snake bites. It's up to Detective Charles Prentice to solve the case in this British-made horror.

Fun Facts:

The family whose house is burned down is called the Addersons, named after a snake, the adder.

BEAST FROM 20,000 FATHOMS - 1953

Long before *Jurassic Park* there was *The Beast from 20,000 Fathoms*. A feat of special effects, this story of an unthawed dinosaur is ahead of its time.

The film tells the story of a Rhedosaurus awoken from the ice during a nuclear bomb test. After it stomps its way south, a team of scientists and military personnel tries to track the beast.

Eventually the Rhedosaurus makes its way to Manhattan to crush cars, eat police officers and cause city-wide panic.

Fun Facts:

20,000 fathoms must be an exaggeration. That works out at around 120,000 feet. The deepest part of the ocean is around 36,800 feet deep.

GAMERA THE GIANT MONSTER - 1965

Unlike Godzilla, Gamera is a giant turtle with the ability to fly and has an insatiable lust for petrol. However, very much like Godzilla, Gamera can breathe fire and has a desire to destroy Tokyo.

This Japanese monster flick follows a team of scientists and a young boy, who shares a sympathetic connection with the beast, as they try to stop the monster from attacking the city.

Fun Facts:

This was the final kaiju movie to be filmed in black and white, and Gamera's only appearance as an antagonist.

THE GIANT GILA MONSTER - 1959

"Have you heard the reports of a giant lizard?"

In the Lone Star state of Texas a series of fatal motor accidents and missing people forces police to begin a major investigation.

They are shocked when their investigation leads to the discovery of a giant lizard roaming the town.

A hot rod-obsessed teen may be the town's only hope against this venomous creature, as the gila monster sets its sights on a local dance hall.

Fun Facts:

A real Mexican Beaded Lizard was used as the onscreen monster. They range from fifty-seven to ninety-one centimetres in length.

THE ALLIGATOR PEOPLE - 1959

"Dirty, stinkin', slimy gators!"

Starring Lon Chaney Jr., *The Alligator People* recounts the tale of a wife whose husband abandons her on a train.

While drugged by two medical professionals, the wife, who has no conscious memory of her husband, recalls the events of her repressed past.

She tells the doctors how, years after her husband's disappearance, she discovered he had been the subject of a horrific experiment which had turned him into some kind of alligator-human hybrid.

Fun Facts:

In 1983 a video game adaptation was produced for the Atari 2600. Sadly it was never properly released.

💀 GODZILLA VS THE WORLD 💀

The King of the Monsters has fought in some epic battles during the course of his film career. Below are the menacing monsters he has faced:

Anguirus

Baragon

Battra

Behemoth

Biollante

Destoroyah

Ebirah

Gabara

Ghidorah

Giant Condor

Giant Octopus

Gigan

Gorosaurus

Hedorah

Jet Jaguar

Kamacuras

King Caesar

King Kong

Kumonga

Manda

Mechagodzilla

Megaguirus

Megalon

Methuselah

M.O.G.U.E.R.A.

Mothra

Mutos

Orga

Rodan

Scylla

Space Godzilla

Titanosaurus

Varan

Zilla

FEARSOME FLYERS

Is it a bird? Is it a plane? No, it's a black and white movie monster!

These winged creatures are few and far between; however, the ones that flew onto the silver screen certainly left an impression.

From feathered behemoths to squeaking bats, the skies of the forties and fifties were not just reserved for alien spacecraft.

Here we look at some of the sky demons that shook the world.

THE DEVIL BAT - 1940

"Now, rub it on the tender part of your neck."

Bela Lugosi stars in the terrifying tale of an inventor and his sick obsession with getting revenge on his previous employers.

After his invention is used to make a huge profit for his bosses, Dr Carruthers produces huge bats and an aftershave that the bats detest.

Ensuring his ex-employers and desired victims douse themselves in the aftershave, Dr Carruthers plans for his giant bats to attack them and get rid of the people he hates.

Fun Facts:

Baby bats are called pups, and a group of bats is known as a colony.

THE FLYING SERPENT - 1946

Another tale of revenge, but this time the creature is a killer bird god known to the Aztecs as Quetzalcoatl.

Unbeknownst to archaeologist Dr Andrew Forbes, the feather of the bird god causes the bird to slaughter whoever has it in their possession.

After accidentally killing his wife and another doctor, the demented Forbes plans to use this knowledge to exact revenge on those who have wronged him in the past.

Fun Facts:

Quetzalcoatl is a creature which actually exists in Aztec mythology. Its name translates as "feathered serpent" and it was believed to have created humanity.

THE GIANT CLAW - 1957

The Giant Claw is certainly one of the strangest creature designs.

When engineer Mitch MacAfee spots some kind of winged UFO he alerts the Air Force. An investigatory team is sent out, but there is no sign of Mitch's strange beast.

The pilots disregard Mitch's claims but, after several more aircraft disappear, the existence of a giant prehistoric bird starts to seem a lot more likely.

Fun Facts:

Sadly, the creature design was heavily mocked at the time of release, being described as "laughable" and "preposterous-looking".

☠ THE BIG BIRDS OF PLANET EARTH ☠

Although the monster featured in *The Giant Claw* may seem unrealistic, prehistoric birds tell us a different story. Below are just a few avian beasts that used to roam the Earth:

Vorombe Titan   Hatzegopteryx   Arambourgiania

BRAINS, BRAINS, BRAINS!

For some reason, the fifties and sixties saw a large number of brain-related horrors creeping their way onto the silver screen.

Crafting some of the most unique and terrifying abominations, these films were a-head of their time.

In this chapter we explore the power of the human and, in some cases, alien mind.

FIEND WITHOUT A FACE - 1958

Brains with spinal cords strangling people are the creatures of choice in this British-made chiller.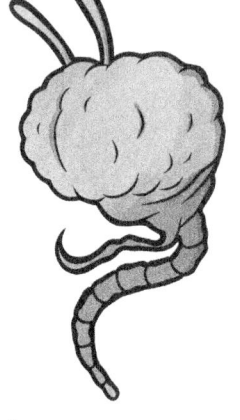

Mind-materialised invisible creatures that feed on atomic power are loose.

After a string of deaths in which the corpses have been rid of their brains and spinal cords, an Air Force Major must investigate.

It is only when these invisible creatures are able to be seen that the Major knows what horrors this town is truly up against.

Fun Facts:

The film was based on a short story called *The Thought Monster*.

THE BRAIN THAT WOULDN'T DIE - 1962

Possibly one of the most haunting monster movies, *The Brain that Wouldn't Die* is a chilling look at life after death.

Dr Cortner believes that there is a way to keep reanimated human body parts alive after death. When his fiancée, Jan, is killed in a car accident, he takes her head to his laboratory and successfully reanimates her.

Jan begs for him to kill her due to the pain, but the doctor plans to find her a body.

Resenting him, Jan telepathically teams up with one of Dr Cortner's previous experiments, who has been locked away in the laboratory cupboard.

Fun Facts:

Although filmed in 1959, it took three years to release the film due to several legal issues.

THE BRAIN FROM PLANET AROUS - 1957

"Well, Earthling. Tomorrow, there will be a new world."

From invisible brains and reanimated heads to giant body-swapping brains from outer space.

Gor, an evil creature from the planet Arous who resembles a huge brain, assumes the identity of a scientist. In the body of Dr Steve March he plans to take over planet Earth.

Meanwhile, another brain from Arous, Val, teams up with Dr March's fiancée to try to put a stop to the interplanetary criminal before it's too late.

Fun Facts:

The contact lenses made for Dr March's evil eye effect were incredibly thick and painful for the actor, John Agar, to wear.

THE BRAIN EATERS - 1958

After the discovery of a large metal structure sticking out of the ground, Senator Walter Powers is sent to investigate.

The residents and authorities of Riverdale, Illinois are acting strange, almost possessed, and townspeople are going missing.

Walter Powers discovers a parasite that attaches itself to the neck of its victims, seemingly taking control of their minds.

With communication to the outside world cut off, Powers must destroy the alien life form and save the world from a hostile takeover.

Fun Facts:

The producers of the film were sued by author Robert A. Heinlein for similarities to his novel *The Puppet Masters*.

CREATURE WITH THE ATOM BRAIN - 1955

"Remote-controlled creatures, their brains powered by atomic energy."

In an attempt to resolve his deportation, gangster Frank Buchanan enlists the aid of Dr Wilhelm Steigg.

Ex-Nazi scientist Steigg is working on a scientific theory that will allow him to control reanimated corpses with voice commands.

Frank helps fund the doctor's work and uses his technology to exact revenge on everyone who has wronged him.

Fun Facts:

A squib is a small explosive, often used with a blood pack to simulate bursting bullet holes on victims. This film is one of the earliest examples of this technique being used.

THE COLOSSUS OF NEW YORK - 1958

Jeremy is a humanitarian with an incredible mind. After winning the Nobel Peace Prize, he is sadly killed in an accident.

His father, a gifted surgeon, keeps his son's brain alive and transplants it into a huge robot body. A robot body with incredible strength, power and laser beams that shoot out of its eyes.

At first Jeremy's kind personality is present, but as time goes on this begins to change, resulting in a very powerful creature with a very dark intention.

Fun Facts:

Ed Wolff, who played Jeremy's robot body, was seven feet tall! He also starred as various monsters and mutants in *The Phantom Creeps*, *Return of the Fly* and *Invaders from Mars*.

DONOVAN'S BRAIN - 1953

Three scientists are researching the brain through experiments on monkeys. Working within his home laboratory, Dr Pat Cory hopes to find the key to sustaining brain life without the human body.

When a private plane crashes near to their home, the sole survivor, a millionaire who is at death's door, is brought to the doctor's lab.

The doctor extracts the millionaire's brain and keeps it alive. Unbeknownst to the doctor, the millionaire is a ruthless and evil man, and his brain has plans to telepathically take over the doctor's body.

Fun Facts:

Orson Welles voiced the character of Dr Cory in the radio play version of *Donovan's Brain*.

THE BRAINIAC - 1962

Known as *El Baron del Terror* in Mexico, its country of origin, *The Brainiac* tells the tale of a seventeenth century Baron who is burned at the stake.

During the Baron's execution a comet passes overhead. As it does, the Baron vows to return when the next comet passes and wreak revenge on the descendants of his persecutors.

We fast-forward to modern-day Mexico where, as promised, the Baron returns with a host of powers. This includes the ability to turn into hairy, forked-tongue beast that can suck the brain out of its victims.

Fun Facts:

Abel Salazar, who played the Baron, was a well-respected actor in the Mexican horror genre.

☠ TYPEFACES OF DEATH ☠

One thing that is fondly appreciated in the world of B-Movies and Creature Features is the posters.

The screaming heroine and the monsters themselves may well have played an important part; however, the dramatic fonts and larger than life typefaces had a pivotal role in monster movie marketing.

Let's have a look at some of the ghoulish fonts that graced these putrid posters.

LEECHES

KING

PHANTOM

HOUSE

WASP

MAN-MADE MONSTERS

If the black and white creature features have taught us anything, it is that the true monsters are human.

In this chapter we look at the ghastly and devastating results of experiments gone wrong, deals with the devil and men playing God.

Whether it be for greed, knowledge or vanity, these characters learnt their lesson the horrifyingly hard way.

FRANKENSTEIN - 1931

The story of the most famous man-made monster was penned by Mary Shelley at the age of just twenty-one.

This Universal Pictures adaptation gave both Boris Karloff and Colin Clive their most celebrated and remembered performances.

The film tells the story of Dr Frankenstein as he tries to create life from various dead body parts.

The doctor succeeds in his mission, but his monster ventures out of the lab and has trouble understanding his mind, purpose and strength.

The villagers don't believe in Frankenstein playing God and look to put a stop to the monster and its creator.

Fun Facts:

Boris Karloff's character is simply credited as **?**

MAN-MADE MONSTER - 1941

Lon Chaney Jr. stars as Dan McCormick. After being the sole survivor of a tragic accident, it appears he is immune to deadly electricity.

Dr Lawrence, interested in Dan's ability to conduct the electrical charge and avoid electrocution, asks him to come to his lab.

Secretly, Dr Lawrence's colleague, a mad scientist by the name of Dr Rigas, has plans of his own.

Upping the flow of electricity into Dan's body, the mad scientist leaves Dan's mind fried with superhuman electrical powers, perfect for the mad scientist to control for his own evil doings.

Fun Facts:

Lon Chaney Jr. has played Frankenstein's Monster, The Wolfman, Count Dracula and The Mummy.

THE PICTURE OF DORIAN GRAY - 1945

 Based on the Oscar Wilde novel, this film tells the story of Dorian Gray, a handsome and wealthy aristocrat.

After having his portrait painted, he wishes that the painting could grow old instead of him.

As he begins to lead a life of sin and selfishness, the painting changes, becoming ugly and disfigured. Dorian believes his wish may have come true.

Dorian locks the painting away and continues his ageless living, but his soul may be just as ugly as his portrait.

Fun Facts:

Dorian's love interest is played by Angela Lansbury.

THE HIDEOUS SUN DEMON - 1958

An accident leads scientist Gilbert McKenna to be exposed to high levels of radiation. Doctors are baffled that McKenna is seemingly unharmed.

After receiving treatment in a solarium, harnessing the healing power of the sun's rays, McKenna transforms into a hideous lizard-like beast.

It is quickly discovered that McKenna only becomes the lizard when in direct contact with sunlight.

Slowly, as McKenna tries to keep himself in the dark, the lizard's murderous thoughts begin taking over.

Fun Facts:

This was the first film of Nan Peterson, who went on to appear in *Rawhide*, *Gunsmoke*, *Perry Mason,* and *The Twilight Zone.*

BRIDE OF FRANKENSTEIN - 1935

"We belong dead."

Universal's sequel to *Frankenstein* starts with Elsa Lanchester playing author Mary Shelley, who says that there is more story to tell.

Dr Frankenstein and his creation have both survived the events of the first film. The doctor quickly returns to his work with the aid of his former mentor Dr Pretorius.

Meanwhile, the monster learns to speak, with the teachings of a blind old man who accepts the creature as a normal human.

The doctor is forced to create a mate, also played by Elsa Lanchester, for the monster.

Fun Facts:

Boris Karloff didn't want the monster to speak.

☠ KARLOFF AND LANCHESTER ☠

The Bride of Frankenstein has to be one of my all-time favourites. The pairing of Boris Karloff and Elsa Lanchester is perfect and has created a tragic horror love story that has become nothing short of iconic.

Elsa Lanchester was born in London, England in 1902. She studied dance and went on to perform in cabaret and theatre at a young age.

After moving to the United States of America, Elsa began starring in short films, eventually being cast in feature-length productions.

Although appearing in over sixty films throughout her career, Lanchester didn't dabble with the horror genre anywhere near as much as her co-star, Boris Karloff.

Lanchester sadly died in 1986, aged eighty-four.

Almost one hundred years before Elsa Lanchester's tragic passing, a young man by the name of William Pratt was born.

William Pratt took the stage name of Boris Karloff after he began acting on stage in Canada.

Although Frankenstein's monster may be Karloff's most famous role, he had actually appeared in over eighty films prior to this.

Karloff went on to star in many creature features and is celebrated as one of the biggest names in horror.

Boris Karloff sadly passed away on February 2nd, 1969 and was laid to rest at the Guildford Crematorium in Surrey, England.

THE KILLER SHREWS - 1959

"Why, that's as big as a full-grown wolf!"

A scientist, looking to help with the world's overpopulation, is experimenting with shrinking humans on a remote island.

Sadly his experiments lead him to accidentally create a colony of giant shrews.

Due to a hurricane, a group are trapped on the island and must fend off the poisonous, blood-thirsty creatures.

Fun Facts:

Actor James Best returned as Thorne Sherman in a sequel, entitled *Return of the Killer Shrews*, in 2012. With a 53-year gap, it is one of the longest between film sequels in history.

THE INVISIBLE MAN - 1933

Another one from Universal Pictures, 1933's *The Invisible Man* stars Claude Rains as the titular character.

Rains plays Dr Jack Griffin, who manages to turn himself invisible. Wrapped in bandages and scarves to hide his affliction, he checks into a pub's guest room.

After not paying his bill, being angry with the staff and making a mess with his experiments, he is asked to leave.

The mild-mannered Dr Griffin slowly becomes more maniacal and more deadly as he plots to enact a reign of terror.

Fun Facts:

Claude Rains also played the Phantom in Universal's adaptation of *The Phantom of the Opera*.

SON OF INGAGI - 1940

This American-made monster flick was the first science fiction movie to feature an all-black cast.

It tells the tale of a couple who inherit a house from a doctor who had recently returned from a trip to Africa.

Sadly for the Lindsays, the doctor brought back a monster named N'Gina, who is living inside the gloomy old house with them.

Money, mystery and murder are all to be found in this chilling creature feature.

Fun Facts:

The monster's name, N'Gina, translates as "One Who Serves" in the Kenyan language, Kikuyu.

DAY THE WORLD ENDED - 1955

"Our story begins with... the end!"

Shot in around nine days, *Day the World Ended* is a post-apocalyptic movie about a disjointed group of townsfolk trying to survive.

The world has been ravaged by nuclear war, and radioactive mutated humans are scattered across the land.

In amongst the group of survivors are a geologist, a rancher and a troubled couple of criminals. Together they must keep the peace and fight off a terrifying horned creature.

Fun Facts:

The character of Louise keeps a picture of her late boyfriend by her bed. The photo is actually a picture of director Roger Corman.

BRIDE OF THE MONSTER - 1955

Our first film by the king of the B-movies himself, Ed Wood, is *Bride of the Monster*

It tells the tale of a doctor, played by Bela Lugosi, as he tries to create super-human monsters with atomic power.

A reporter by the name of Janet Lawton investigates, trying to connect the doctor's work with a spate of missing people in the area.

Sadly, after swerving off the road, the reporter is captured by the doctor's giant mute assistant, Lobo.

Tensions mount as the police try to save Janet and stop the doctor's plans.

Fun Facts:

Lobo was played by actor and professional wrestler Tor Johnson, who wrestled under the name Thor.

THE INVISIBLE MAN RETURNS - 1940

Universal Pictures' sequel to *The Invisible Man* stars Vincent Price as Geoffrey Radcliffe. Radcliffe has been wrongfully imprisoned and is awaiting execution for the "murder" of his brother.

The brother of Claude Rains' character from the original film gives Radcliffe a drug that will turn him invisible.

With his newfound transparency, Radcliffe is able to escape prison, but the drug has a side effect - gradual insanity.

Fun Facts:

The film was nominated for an Academy Award for its visual effects.

MONSTER ON THE CAMPUS - 1958

A ghastly neanderthal is the monster of choice in this American horror.

Dr Blake is excited to receive a prehistoric fish specimen for his research. Whilst examining the partially-thawed fish he accidentally catches his skin on its tooth.

The contamination of the fish blood causes living creatures to devolve into a more primitive state, due to the fish's contact with gamma radiation.

The doctor discovers that he himself has been reverting into a murderous caveman-like creature and trashing the campus.

Fun Facts:

The Pokémon Relicanth is based on the coelacanth, the fish being studied by Dr Blake.

THE AMAZING TRANSPARENT MAN - 1960

"My aim is to make an entire army invisible."

More see-through shenanigans as an ex-Army Major, Paul Kenner, works with a doctor to achieve complete invisibility.

His plan is to make an army of invisible soldiers and sell the idea to the highest bidder.

In order to obtain more radium for the experiments, Kenner enlists the help of criminal safecracker Joey Faust.

Kenner soon discovers that invisible convicts are not to be trusted.

Fun Facts:

A Canadian company has patented the technology behind a material that bends light to make people and objects almost invisible to the naked eye.

💀 HALLOWEEN AS THE INVISIBLE MAN 💀

Stuck for a Halloween costume? The Invisible Man is a great look for a small price. Here's the accessories you'll need:

Bandages   Sunglasses

Hat   Gloves

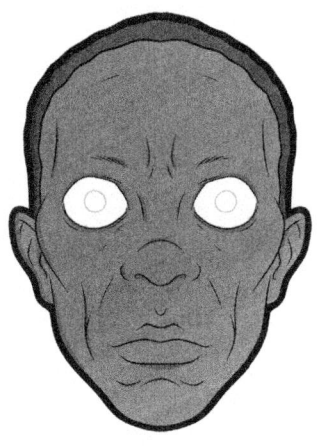

UNDEAD ON ARRIVAL

Through every decade of black and white cinema, the silver screen has been haunted by ghastly ghouls and gruesome ghosts.

Perhaps it's our inherent fear of life after death that keeps us fascinated by morbid stories of spectres and spirits.

From Egyptian Mummies to Caribbean Zombies to American Apparitions, this chapter looks at the undead in a wide variety of styles, shapes and sizes.

THE MUMMY – 1932

Imhotep, played by Boris Karloff, is an ancient high priest who is hoping to resurrect his dead lover. Sadly, for his dabbling in the dark arts, he is condemned and buried alive.

In 1921 his mummified remains are unearthed along with the Scroll of Thoth, used for resurrecting the dead. When a member of the expedition reads the text aloud, they awaken Imhotep and go insane in the process.

A decade later, the mummy sees a woman who he believes is his reincarnated love, and tries to make her his bride forever.

Fun Facts:

The film has spawned many sequels, remakes and reboots such as *The Mummy's Hand* and *The Mummy's Tomb*.

13 GHOSTS - 1960

Released in "Illusion-O", *13 Ghosts* had its own special viewer (similar to 3D glasses) that allowed the audience to see the ghosts.

The story follows a family as they inherit a large house. The downside is that the house is haunted by the previous owner's collection of ghosts.

Looking through their own special viewers, the family sees all kinds of apparitions, from headless lion tamers to flaming skeletons.

Hearing that their family member's fortune lays hidden somewhere in the house, the new residents try to find the treasure before something evil finds them.

Fun Facts:

The lion seen with the lion tamer ghost was named Zamba. He also starred in The Addams Family.

💀 ILLUSION-O AND HOW IT WORKED 💀

Members of the audience were given special viewers for the film's cinema release. Each special viewer had a red and blue cellophane viewing panel.

The red panel was named "The Ghost Viewer" and the blue panel was named "The Ghost Remover".

Cinema-goers could choose whether or not they wanted to see the ghosts by choosing a panel at specific parts of the film.

This was achieved by having blue-tinted backgrounds with red-tinted apparitions floating around.

The corresponding coloured panels would cancel out the coloured footage, either leaving just the ghosts or just the background.

Cinema-goers were given a briefing before the movie started. It was stated that the special viewers were left behind by Dr Zorba and that the audience should use them when the characters in the film put their ghost viewers on.

Ultimately it was a fun gimmick to promote the film and give its viewers a unique experience.

Director William Castle was notorious for creative gimmicks that helped market his movies, earning him the nickname "King of the Gimmicks".

The Tingler saw some cinema seats have a vibrating mechanism to replicate the on-screen creature attacking its victim.

I WALKED WITH A ZOMBIE - 1943

Far from the brain-craving, rotten creatures of the modern zombie movie, *I Walked with a Zombie* deals with voodoo on the island of Saint Sebastian.

A nurse gets a job on a Caribbean island, looking after the ill wife of a sugar plantation owner. The lady is apparently mute and emotionless after a severe case of tropical fever attacks her spinal cord.

After trying everything else, the nurse takes the ill woman to a voodoo priest. There a man in black stabs the ill woman, who doesn't bleed.

Whispers fill the voodoo temple, saying that the afflicted woman is actually a zombie.

Fun Facts:

The shooting time for the film was cut by five days. This was due to wartime gasoline rationing.

THE HAUNTING - 1963

"God! God! Whose hand was I holding?"

Hill House is apparently haunted. A morbid history of horrific deaths and insanity plagues the old mansion.

His interest piqued, Dr Markway decides to visit the home with the sceptical young heir who stands to inherit it, a clairvoyant, and a nervous psychic.

Together they plan to disprove the existence of ghosts and the curse of Hill House; however, they soon find out there is a lot more truth in the tales than they bargained for.

Fun Facts:

Director Steven Spielberg once said that *The Haunting* was one of the scariest movies ever made.

THE GHOUL - 1933

This British horror, starring Boris Karloff, tells the tale of Professor Henry Morlant.

Morlant is an Egyptologist who believes that a jewel in his possession holds the key to resurrection and rejuvenation.

After suffering from a disfiguring ailment, Morlant dies. Before his passing he requests that the jewel is bandaged to his hand and buried with him in his Egyptian-style tomb. He states that a curse will be put upon those who try to steal the jewel.

Lo and behold, a robber breaks into the tomb and takes Morlant's prized possession. Morlant rises from the dead to enact revenge on his wrong-doers.

Fun Facts:

This was the first British horror film to have sound.

WHITE ZOMBIE - 1932

A loving couple is talked into hosting their wedding at a friend's plantation in Haiti. Unbeknownst to the couple, Monsieur Beaumont, the plantation owner, is secretly in love with the bride-to-be.

With seemingly no way of capturing the girl's heart, Beaumont reaches out to the treacherous Lengendre, played by Bela Lugosi.

Lengendre, who uses mind control to turn people in emotionless zombies, turns his attention to the bride-to-be, with devastating results.

Fun Facts:

Musician and horror director Rob Zombie named his first band after this film.

HOUSE ON HAUNTED HILL - 1959

"What husband hasn't, at some time, wanted to kill his wife?"

Another haunted house flick starring the phenomenal Vincent Price was released just one year prior to *13 Ghosts*.

House on Haunted Hill tells the tale of five money-hungry locals who are invited by a millionaire to spend the night in his home.

Along with the millionaire and his wife, the five must survive the night in the supposedly haunted house to earn themselves a cool ten thousand dollars.

Fun Facts:

In the 1999 remake, Geoffrey Rush's millionaire character is named Mr Price as a tribute to Vincent Price, who had passed away six years prior.

THE SCREAMING SKULL - 1958

Eric and Jenni, a pair of newlyweds, arrive at the husband's desolate mansion. Eric's first wife, Marianne, sadly died in the house after a freak accident.

Jenni starts to see strange things and believes that her mental illnesses are worsening. One of her visions is of a skull that may or may not be her imagination.

As Jenni battles with her paranoia, it is clear that the gardener maintaining the property holds Marianne in deep regard.

Suspicions are high in this American-made mystery.

Fun Facts:

The director of the film, Alex Nicol, also played Mickey the gardener.

OUT OF THIS WORLD

From grave-robbing aliens to one-eyed octopuses, many of the silver screen's most famous monsters came from a planet beyond the stars.

Before 1961 humans had not been to space, and imaginations were running wild. Writers and designers tried to speculate what horrid creatures were hovering just outside our atmosphere.

In this chapter we look at the things from other worlds and their diabolical plans to take over the Earth, or simply put an end to it.

EARTH VS. THE FLYING SAUCERS - 1956

This American-made movie from Columbia Pictures tells the story of aliens coming to Earth after their own solar system has begun to fall apart.

After spotting the first UFO, Dr Marvin reluctantly reports the sighting to his superiors.

It is revealed that several research satellites launched as part of the American Space Program have inexplicably fallen back to Earth.

Suspecting alien interference, Dr Marvin's suspicions are confirmed when a UFO lands at the space program base.

The aliens are met with a hostile attack and for this the Earth will suffer.

Fun Facts:

Stop-motion artist Ray Harryhausen provided the special effects for the UFOs and the crumbling monuments that really make this picture special.

THE CRAWLING EYE - 1958

Also known at *The Trollenberg Terror*, *The Crawling Eye* is a British horror set on the Swiss mountains.

A strange cloud has appeared near a resort hotel and seasoned climbers are mysteriously being decapitated.

An unlikely team of mind readers, journalists, and United Nations representatives, embarks on a rescue mission to find more missing climbers.

Sadly for them, telepathic alien beings are living inside the radioactive cloud, and they aren't friendly.

Fun Facts:

The film was actually a feature length movie remake of a TV miniseries called *The Trollenberg Terror*.

PLAN 9 FROM OUTER SPACE - 1959

Grave robbers from outer space! The second movie from director Ed Wood in this compendium is certainly his most famous.

Often cited as "the worst movie ever made", the film is filled with mistakes, but holds an unparalleled charm.

The film follows Jeff Trent, a pilot who spots a UFO during one of his flights, and a group of police officers trying to uncover the mysteries of murdered gravediggers and missing bodies.

Aliens, led by Commander Eros, are stealing bodies to help make an army of the undead. It's up to Jeff and the police to thwart "Plan 9".

Fun Facts:

The ghoulish widow was played by Hollywood TV personality Maila "Vampira" Nurmi.

Edward D. Wood Jr. is famed for his micro-budget movies and his uncanny ability to obtain opportunities out of thin air.

Often using ridiculous methods, Ed Wood was able to raise funds and get movie deals for his outrageous scripts.

He would then shoot the film cheaply, quickly and often in locations without the required permits. He would continuously ignore mistakes and focus solely on getting the movie finished to make his vision a reality. To do this, Ed Wood would use an unusual array of friends, family and obscure personalities to fill his roles.

It was this tenacity and drive that eventually gave Ed Wood a cult following and his own biopic, starring Johnny Depp and directed by Tim Burton.

Below are ten weird and wonderful facts about *"the worst director of all time"*:

#1 - To obtain funding from the Baptist Church in Los Angeles, Ed convinced many of the cast members to get baptised. The church was unaware at the time that they were funding a film with the working title *Grave Robbers from Outer Space*.

#2 - In 1952 Ed began dating actor and singer Dolores Fuller. After their relationship ended Dolores went on to write songs for Elvis Presley.

#3 - Ed served in the United States Marine Corps just months after the attack on Pearl Harbour. He was assigned to the Second Defence Battalion and reached the rank of Corporal.

#4 - For *Plan 9 from Outer Space* Ed used previously-filmed footage of Bela Lugosi outside his home. Lugosi actually died before production began, so Ed got his chiropractor to play Bela's character and hold a cape over his face.

#5 - When writing, Ed used a number of pen names. These included Ann Gora and Akdov Telmig (which was his favourite drink spelled backwards).

#6 - The University of Southern California began holding an annual Ed Wood Film Festival in 1997. Student teams are challenged to write, film, and edit an Ed Wood-inspired short film based on a preassigned theme.

#7 - Ed supposedly bit the heads off live chickens while working in a carnival sideshow.

#8 - For *Plan 9 from Outer Space* Ed hired a TV psychic named The Amazing Criswell to serve as the narrator. Criswell was famous for his terribly inaccurate predictions.

#9 - Ed held a wake following the funeral of his good friend Kenne Duncan. At the wake he encouraged the attendees to stand on the diving board of his apartment's pool and recount tales of their time with Kenne.

#10 - Although strictly frowned upon at the time, Ed like to dress in women's clothing. His favourite item of clothing was an Angora sweater that he claimed helped him write better scripts. This inspired his film *Glen or Glenda?* but sadly cost him several relationships.

IT CONQUERED THE WORLD - 1956

"You think you're gonna make a slave of the world?
I'll see you in hell first!"

Aliens from Venus come to Earth with the intention of extinguishing emotions in order to bring peace to the planet.

Dr Anderson believes the aliens and agrees to help them with their plan. Little does the doctor know, the aliens' true intentions are much darker, and a full scale takeover is closer to the truth.

The doctor's friends must convince him of the alien's plan and try to stop them before it's too late.

Fun Facts:

Dr Anderson actor Lee Van Cleef went on to star in *The Good, the Bad and the Ugly* with Clint Eastwood.

THE CREEPING TERROR - 1964

"My God! What is it?"

A creeping rug-like monster that eats its victims and leaves their shoes is possibly the most bizarre creature in our compendium.

In this TV movie a newlywed sheriff has to protect his town after a long fuzzy alien-being lurches from its spaceship.

Seemingly hungry for teenage music lovers, the alien crawls its way to a dance hall, where the sheriff must do anything he can to stop this carnivorous carpet monster and keep his wife safe.

Fun Facts:

Rumour has it, due to a pay dispute, the original creature costume was stolen a day before shooting began. A poorly constructed replica was made.

THE THING FROM ANOTHER WORLD - 1951

Based on the novella *Who Goes There?* by John W Campbell, this film follows a group of scientists at an Arctic research station as they find a UFO trapped in the ice.

Noticing a frozen lifeform in the pilot's seat, the team decides to take the specimen back to their station.

Their high spirits are dampened when the creature is accidentally thawed out.

Fun Facts:

Who Goes There? also inspired 1982 horror *The Thing*, starring Kurt Russell.

The film contains one of the first full-body fire stunts ever filmed.

IT CAME FROM OUTER SPACE - 1953

When an alien spacecraft crashes to Earth, stargazer John and his girlfriend Ellen are the only two people to catch a glimpse.

John investigates further and, before a landslide covers all evidence, sees the alien spacecraft and its terrifying occupant.

John and Ellen try to tell the sheriff about the creature from outer space, but he doesn't believe them.

When the townsfolk start acting strange, the amateur stargazer is convinced the alien is behind it.

Fun Facts:

This was the first 3-D film to be released by Universal Studios and was one of the few movies from the 1950s to have its credits at the end of the picture.

THE MONOLITH MONSTERS - 1957

"Look at the dog - it's as hard as a piece of granite!"

More crash landing aliens, this time in the form of a black meteorite that explodes into hundreds of strange black rocks.

When a storm exposes the alien rocks to water, they grow into huge monoliths that topple and multiply upon breaking.

Any humans or animals that are in the way are crushed or turned to stone.

The townsfolk must put an end to this alien invasion before the world is overrun by the Monolith Monsters.

Fun Facts:

Growing stones too farfetched? Actually, there are real stones named Trovants that move and grow.

THE DAY THE EARTH STOOD STILL - 1951

An intergalactic ambassador named Klaatu lands his spacecraft in Washington D.C. The purpose of his interplanetary voyage is to deliver an ultimatum.

Guarded by an eight-foot robot named Gort, Klaatu leaves his spaceship and asks to speak to the world's leaders. The request is declined due to the ongoing war.

After speaking with a brilliant scientist named Professor Barnhardt, Klaatu explains that he must destroy the Earth in a bid to save other planets from the human race's destructive actions, unless the earthlings are willing to change.

Fun Facts:

In the short story *Farewell to the Master* that the film is based on, Gort is called Gnut and Klaatu dies pretty early on.

I MARRIED A MONSTER FROM OUTER SPACE - 1958

"If it weren't so silly, I'd say you were Bill's twin brother from another place."

The night before his wedding day, Bill leaves his bachelor party to head home. On his way he sees a body lying in the road.

He stops his car but, whilst investigating, is grabbed by a glowing alien who steals his identity and takes his place at the ceremony.

The wedding goes ahead, but his new bride starts noticing some very strange behaviour from her once loving and compassionate husband.

Fun Facts:

The dogs that attack the aliens were frightened of the costumes. To overcome this, the dogs spent time with the actors; however, this worked too well and the dogs just wanted to play with the aliens afterwards.

DEVIL GIRL FROM MARS - 1954

"Come. I will show you wonders you have never
seen before."

This British sci-fi flick tells the tale of Nyah, a female Martian who is forced to perform an emergency landing whilst on her way to London.

Nyah lands in Scotland and is accompanied by her robot guard Chani, and armed with a ray gun. She explains that she is visiting Earth to capture men.

It seems that a war of the sexes on Mars has resulted in a lack of good quality males for breeding. Nyah is looking for some superior breeding stock to take back home.

Fun Facts:

Nyah's costume was hot and uncomfortable to wear.

IT! THE TERROR FROM BEYOND SPACE - 1958

Fiend Without a Face star Marshall Thompson heads up this sci-fi horror about the first manned space mission to Mars.

After his spacecraft returns to Earth, Colonel Carruthers is suspected of killing the other nine members of his crew while they were on Mars.

Carruthers denies this, and blames the deaths on a horrid creature from the Red Planet who has climbed into the ship and is still on board.

Fun Facts:

This final battle scene of this movie is showing at the drive-in in the music video for *Summer of '69* by Bryan Adams.

💀 INTERPLANETARY TRAVEL TIMES 💀

Ever wondered how long it would take to reach another planet?

Firstly, we'll assume that you've calculated when your chosen planet is at its closest position to Earth within its own orbit. That's just sensible planning.

Secondly, we'll base our travel speeds on the New Horizons spacecraft, which is one of the fastest human-made objects ever built!

Mercury

"The Swift Planet"

Distance: 48 million miles

Estimated Travel Time: 40 days

Venus

"The Evening Star"

Distance: 38 million miles

Estimated Travel Time: 32 days

Mars

"The Red Planet"

Distance: 51 million miles

Estimated Travel Time: 43 days

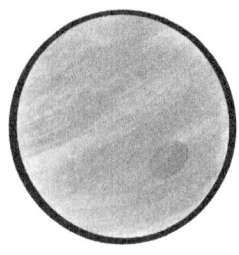

Jupiter

"The Gas Giant"

Distance: 367 million miles

Estimated Travel Time: 306 days

Saturn

"The Ringed Planet"

Distance: 746 million miles

Estimated Travel Time: 622 days

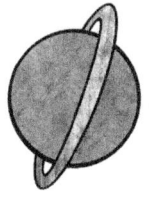

Uranus

"The Bulls-Eye Planet"

Distance: 1.7 billion miles

Estimated Travel Time: 1416 days

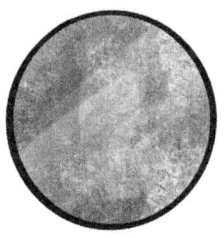

Neptune

"The Blue Giant"

Distance: 2.7 billion miles

Estimated Travel Time: 2250 days

MISSILE TO THE MOON - 1958

This American-made creature feature tells the story of scientist Dirk Green's journey to the moon.

Unbeknownst to the scientist, two escaped convicts, his lab partner and his fiancée are all on board.

During the trip Dirk is killed, leaving the four stowaways to complete the landing.

Once on the moon, the unlikely foursome must overcome the horrors of an underground civilisation ruled by the sinister Lido, a cave-dwelling spider and bipedal rock creatures.

Fun Facts:

The film is actually a remake of the movie *Cat-Women of the Moon* (1953).

INVASION OF THE BODY SNATCHERS - 1956

A secret invasion is quietly underway in this American sci-fi picture. Alien plant spores have made their way to Earth and are growing into large seed pods.

The pods have the ability to duplicate any human they come in contact with, eventually learning their memories, personalities and characteristics.

Dr Bennell must uncover the secret before everyone is a doppelgänger.

Fun Facts:

The film's body snatching theme is based on the Capgras delusion. Capgras delusion, or Capgras syndrome, is a psychiatric disorder in which a person holds the delusion that a friend, spouse, parent, or other close family member has been replaced by an identical impostor.

THE BEAST WITH 1,000,000 EYES - 1955

"They shall be my ears, my eyes, until your world is mine!"

On a remote desert ranch, the Kelley family witnesses some kind of aircraft crash nearby. Suddenly, the domestic and wild animals near the ranch begin to act strangely and end up trying to attack the family.

The family suspects the aircraft may be part of an alien takeover when a friendly local farmer turns on them.

The beast from another world is able to see through the eyes of lesser creatures, and it has its sights on the Kelley family.

Fun Facts:

Duke the dog was played by a dog named London.

VILLAGE OF THE DAMNED - 1960

A wave of unconsciousness falls on a small English village. After several hours the residents wake up, but something has changed.

All of the women capable of bearing a child are mysteriously pregnant. When the women give birth, the children are all born with bright blonde hair and piercing eyes.

As they grow up, at an alarming rate, it is clear these children have the power to make people do things they don't want to do.

Fun Facts:

The film is based on a novel called *The Midwich Cuckoos,* named for the cuckoo bird that often lays its eggs in the nests of other unsuspecting birds, which then raise the hatchlings as their own.

NOT OF THIS EARTH - 1957

An alien invader on a cosmic mission for blood is the foe in this feverish flick. *Not of this Earth* tells the story of an alien race trying to fix its war-torn planet, Davanna.

Sadly for the Earthlings, it's human blood the aliens need, as theirs has been polluted by nuclear fallout.

The alien researcher, known as Mr Johnson, maims and kills with his fatal white-eyed stare in order to collect blood samples.

Fun Facts:

Paul Birch, who played the alien, apparently walked off set before the film was finished. Another actor had to be brought in to act as a body double.

ROBOT MONSTER - 1953

The extraterrestrial robot named Ro-Man has managed to destroy most of Earth's inhabitants.

Just a handful of people are immune to his death ray, and are desperate to survive.

The film follows Ro-Man as he tries to annihilate the last few survivors, but things get complicated with the creature falls for a young female Earthling.

Fun Facts:

The film was shot and released in 3-D. It did surprisingly well and managed to gross sixty-two times its budget.

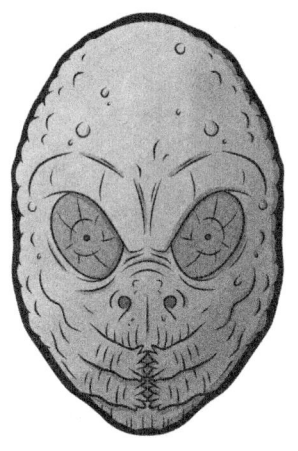

MISCELLANEOUS MONSTERS

Alas, we are nearing the end of this colossal compendium of carnivorous creatures. In this chapter we explore the hideous and hostile monsters that refuse to sit in any one category.

From shuffling tree beasts to mole men from beneath the soil, these critters are some of the more obscure and ghastly to grace the silver screen.

MAN BEAST - 1956

An explorer goes missing whilst searching for the fabled Yeti. His sister, Connie Hayward, sets off on an exhibition into the Himalayan Mountains to try to find him.

During their search, Connie and her team stumble across a strange old guide named Vargas.

It isn't long before the legendary Yeti is spotted and the team is attacked.

Connie must survive the cold and the attack of the Abominable Snowman.

Fun Facts:

The director of the film, Jerry Warren, married his partner, British cinematographer Brianne Murphy, right after finishing *Man Beast*. During their honeymoon he penned his next film, *Teenage Zombies*.

FROM HELL IT CAME - 1957

"In death, I will be stronger than you in life!"

A vengeful tree monster named Tabanga is on the loose in this sci-fi horror.

After a prince is wrongfully executed for the murder of his father, he is resurrected as a shuffling, sour-faced tree stump.

In an attempt to enact revenge, the tree monster stalks the islanders. Meanwhile, a group of American doctors has come to the island to help with a suspected plague outbreak.

Little do they know, the plague is the last of their worries.

Fun Facts:

It is rumoured that Marvel co-creator Stan Lee got his inspiration for the character Groot from this film.

THE SLIME PEOPLE – 1963

A thick fog has engulfed Los Angeles. A string of underground atomic tests has disturbed a subterranean race of reptile-like creatures.

Reported as "Slime People" due to their gooey skin, the newly discovered race uses a strange fog to cut the city off from the outside world.

A pilot is forced to land in L.A. and finds he is one of a handful willing to save the planet.

Fun Facts:

Director and star Robert Hutton borrowed his father-in-law's real-life butcher shop for the butcher shop and freezer scenes.

THE LAND UNKNOWN - 1957

The U.S. Navy arranges an expedition into Antartica for Commander Roberts, two of his men and a female reporter.

A catastrophic crash causes the pilot to conduct an emergency landing straight into a volcanic crater. Inside they find a tropical jungle filled with carnivorous plants and dinosaurs.

Things only get worse when the insane survivor of a previous expedition kidnaps the reporter.

The only way out alive is fixing their damaged vessel before it's too late.

Fun Facts:

Jack Arnold, director of *Creature from the Black Lagoon*, was originally going to direct this film. Sadly, budget cuts forced him to leave the project.

BEAST FROM HAUNTED CAVE - 1959

A group of thieves plans to steal a large amount of gold from a bank. To cause a distraction whilst the heist is carried out, one of the criminals is sent to a local mine to set off an explosive.

The explosion wakes a multi-limbed beast that attacks one of the crew.

Ignoring the dangers, the thieves hire a local guide named Gil Jackson and set off to a remote cabin to catch their getaway plane.

Gil is unaware of the criminal activity, but gets roped into a tale of love, betrayal and beastly encounters.

Fun Facts:

During some of the scenes guns were fired inside a real abandoned mine. This caused part of the ceiling to collapse. Luckily, no one was hurt.

THE ABOMINABLE SNOWMAN - 1957

"There is no Yeti!"

This Hammer horror, starring Peter Cushing, follows a team of scientists as they explore the Himalayas in search for the legendary Yeti.

When large footprints are found, the team is sure of the Yeti's existence.

The band of unlikely companions searches the area, but a bear trap injures one of the scientists, leading them to stop for a moment.

The team can't wait to get back to their search, but sadly for them, the creature they are looking for has already found them.

Fun Facts:

Peter Cushing starred in this film and the BBC television play *The Creature* on which it was based.

💀 THE PETRIFYING PETER CUSHING 💀

My first encounter with the incredible Peter Cushing was Hammer Horror's *The Curse of Franskenstein*. Cushing plays Victor Frankenstein in his first leading role and does not disappoint.

The English actor was born on May 26th 1913. After seeing a stage production of Peter Pan, he gained an interest in acting.

Cushing went on to star in numerous horror classics such as *The Gorgon*, *The Mummy*, *Dr. Terror's House of Horrors*, as well as a host of Frankenstein sequels.

One of Cushing's most famous returning roles was as Van Helsing, often seen battling fellow horror legend Christopher Lee as Dracula.

Cushing sadly died on August 11th 1994 at the age of eighty-one.

THE MOLE PEOPLE - 1956

An earthquake during an archaeological dig in Asia leads to the discovery of a hidden ancient world.

Exploring further, the scientists discover an underground society. The subterranean city is occupied by Sumerian albinos, who have adapted to living underground but use humanoid mole men as slaves.

The Sumerians believe that the scientists are messengers from their goddess. However, Dr Bentley worries what will happen when they find out they aren't.

Fun Facts:

Real moles are insectivores, meaning they usually eat worms, insects, grubs and slugs... Yuck!

CAT PEOPLE - 1942

From Slime People to Mole People to Cat People! This American horror tells the tale of Irena Dubrovna, a Serbian artist who has moved to America.

She falls in love, but believes she may be holding on to a deadly secret.

Irena is preoccupied with the notion that she is descended from an ancient tribe who turn into large cats when passionate, jealous or angry.

Her fears become an obsession as she and her new husband try to uncover the dark mystery of Irena's paranoia.

Fun Facts:

The film features a jump scare technique known as a "Lewton Bus", named after the movie's producer Val Lewton.

☠ THAT'S A WRAP ☠

Well, my friends, there you have it. A colossal compendium of silver screen scares and Hollywood horrors.

Although flawed, these films hold a very special place in my heart. They were made with passion, creativity and wild imagination.

They dared question what lurked within our oceans, who lived beyond the stars, and what monstrosities science could create.

At a time when people feared atomic war and nuclear devastation, these filmmakers made art, overcoming budget restraints, prop thefts, and even cast members dying, to achieve their goals.

These films were made in black and white, but the creatures and characters are some of the most colourful and diverse to ever to grace our cinema screens.

With tales of heroism, tragedy, camaraderie, they taught us that, by working together, we could overcome any challenge the universe threw at us.

As a kid, laying on the lounge floor with my dad and a big bag of popcorn was my happy place.

Vampira lurking through the graveyard in *Plan 9 From Outer Space*, Gort disintegrating a whole tank in *The Day the Earth Stood Still*, giant grasshoppers climbing a tower block in *Beginning of the End*, these images are fondly and vividly remembered.

My love for horror and movies in general all started here. I hope this book helps you find your favourite monochrome monster and gives you an insight into the Hollywood horrors of yesteryear.

COLOUR CLASSICS

Listed below are a few classic monster movies that were released in colour, but are just too good not to mention.

- The Birds (1963)
- The Blob (1958)
- Dr. Cyclops (1940)
- The Fly (1958)
- Forbidden Planet (1956)
- Ghidorah the Three-Headed Monster (1964)
- The Gorgon (1964)
- House of Wax (1953)
- Jason and the Argonauts (1963)
- Mothra (1961)
- Reptilicus (1961)
- The Phantom of the Opera (1943)
- This Island Earth (1955)

Please note: All of the films curated in this book have been rated by the British Board of Film Classification as 12 or below.

Due to their age, some of the views, actions and cultural depictions within these films may be deemed as offensive.

Viewer discretion is advised, and please seek an adult's permission before watching any of these films unless certified U.

MOVIE INDEX

ABOUT THE AUTHOR

Joey Draper is the author of the *Twisted Tales for Kooky Kids* book series. He grew up in a small village watching 1950's monster movies and reading spooky novels. He now lives with his wife in Bournemouth, England, which also happens to be the final resting place of Mary Shelley, the author of *Frankenstein*.

Printed in Great Britain
by Amazon

45004131R00116